Quickened Dark

Peter McNamara

*Front cover art: James F. Farley III
Design and typesetting: Ted Wojtasik
Proofreader: Bryan Pacheco*

ISBN-13: 978-0998194981
ISBN-10: 0998194980

**SFA
UNIVERSITY
PRESS**

St. Andrews University Press

St. Andrews University
(A Branch of Webber International University)
1700 Dogwood Mile
Laurinburg, NC 28352
press@sa.edu
(910) 277-5310

Also by Peter McNamara

Critics on Wallace Stevens [essays] (1972)

Rhinoceros (1976)

East River Bridge [opera libretto] (1983)

Loneliness of the Palm (1993)

like a perhaps hand (2000)

Sojourn (2006)

Orbits' Crossing (2013, reissue 2016)

Sixteen Poems (2016)

For Jan Robison *and* James F. Farley III
who bring light

CONTENTS

Provençal Summer Night 1

Discernment 2

As Time Goes 4

Defining Moment 6

Damasks 8

Quickened Dark 9

Deferral: Dublin Snug 11

Infernal Night 12

Open Head: Eject 13

Aegean Skirmish 14

No Landscape 16

Always/ Never 17

Sudden Sodden 19

Poteen 20

Solace 22

To an Anole 24

Venereal Soil 25

(Sand)spurs 26

Admiral Motel & Taxidermy 27

The Barn 29

Uncle Joe 31

Pius, My Man 33

"Pricing the Diamond (or Emerald)" 35

On Mozart's Requiem 36

Sparrow at My Doorstep 37

The Meaning of Is 38

Imperative 40

Shame 41

Restoration 42

Hayfield 43

Clarity 45

Caught Breath 47

Lethargy(4/21/13) 49

Falling in Love Again 50

Après-Mike, 2003 51

Assisted Living 52

Diamond Dust 53

Aftermath (Times Sq. Shuttle) 55

Whitney Alfresco 58

Blizzard of '76 60

Clochán (Beehive Huts) 61

Procession 63

in the night of all men I make
a small night for myself
                    —Pablo Neruda

Provençal Summer Night

In the full moon's dusk-toned theatre
glimmers spark massed pines' depths;
the moon—a Matisse cut-out—looms
foreground, fastened against the sky;

grace notes pendant above shadowed
shrubberies, filaments of fog drift like
incense fingering the night—mist
of a thousand myths, of myriad dreams;

moon-etching darkness—black bean stew
on a simmer—soft summer's breath;
a sigh or whisper from one who in sleep
murmurs hints of far stars' intuitions.

Discernment

a furious hunger for simplicity
        —Tomas Traströmer

The hawk-scrambled sky tangles with
clouds tossed in wind's tom-foolery;
stealthy, amnesiac light loiters,
poulticing blights of seasons past
(though spirit stores hard-copy, gusts
etch data in memory). Will chill not
numb our faults' persistent aches?

There's refreshment in searing wind—
what it doesn't savage it may salve:
January's regimen acts astringent to the
wayward, bewildered spirit, shearing
layers of deceit from rimed thought,
cleansing mind (almost) for another
attempt to snag the apple's savor.

***

At the verge of green depths clarity,
yet veiled within (always) the tentative:
deer statue-still scenting the wind
birds converging on migration's hour
leaves tuned to autumn's orchestration
to spew their fireworks against the sky.

In clefts deep in mountains hues spill
for no eye: keener, more vivid perhaps,
tonalities of birdsong, clapperless bells
quickening pulse through brilliant sky,
harmonic to the discerning, that might
sate our furious hunger for simplicity.

As Time Goes

It's always the old song
        the same old story
        love and glory . . .
        jealousy and hate . . .

then comes spring with its ponderables
its protuberances
flamingoes and orange blossoms
        when they migrated
        where they blocked the sky
it rained pink sunrays
        then someone said—
        always does—and they
wound up festooning ladies hats
extinction loomed.

But jealousy and hate?
        how unseasonable
        because unreasonable
(who's that crank behind the scrim?)
        and since your wristband
        now can read your vital signs
who needs gin (it's not just for
        breakfast anymore)?

We have moonlight and vodka
        never out of date

and days grow short when (if)
    you reach September

You don't need to own it—
a case of do or die—
just put it on offer:
it's up to others to take it up.

Defining Moment

This is no season for soaring flights:
November's palette knife builds dove
gray impasto with a tinct of silver
layered across the motif, more sky
dauber than Boudin. Fields reflect
the murk: corn stubble like pickets
bristles from early snowfall. Pockets
of fog rime the perimeter of woods.
Turned soil, deathly sick of the year,
Looks pale and spent; wind, no crop
to break it, stings at ears; noses run.

Only a few root vegetables—graying,
grudging, hang on (and the comic,
incongruous pumpkins). Along here's
a family farm—just there—that kept
a produce stand last summer—closed
now, though I recall a boy of nine or so
who manned the cash box in August,
adult-proud until I questioned him
on a price; he glanced at his mom—
"was I wrong?" in his clouded eyes.

Look, see those two young towheads
running flat out across the stubble
through this sharp bite? Their dad
has set their marks; the older—the one

I recalled—sprints far ahead of his
(three-year-old?) brother. But the

young one's stumbling on behind, legs
pumping more fiercely the farther he's
distanced. There's no quit in that boy.
I'd come back another year if I could:
I'll bet that small boy will have caught—
even passed—his brother. Pride's
forged his mettle—and sibling rivalry.

Damasks

Sinewy cloud bands torque the troubled sky
blood-flecked above roiling gusts.
Light-scatters—apostrophes to autumn—
ride a stream's purling plash between boulders,
slowing where blocked—patient, deliberate to find a way
'til ice and snowpack dam its sluice—while fish plumb deep
pockets calibrating cold hearts to winter's pulse,
counterpointed by a few dry leaves tumbling, eddying
before a biting breeze.

***

Cloud-cast dawn, day's note card envelope—
reflections come like sellers early to market,
like pelicans tilting, gliding the bay. Awhile
they draw near, then veer off, and I lie spent
my pulse flaring—only squirrel scold
or birdcall to break the freighted stillness
as damasked gleanings half illumining/-roiling
times past—regrettably unfulfilled—flee
to nowhere I might hope to reclaim them.

Quickened Dark

Dusk slips into something more comfortable:
ochre and gold co-opt quiet, softening angles;
sunset that flamed—that flared each leaf—
disrobes in its enticing, seductive tease.
Shadows pool. Lacy filigrees—cast off—
ingest the dark as last light slips away.

Enter hollowed-out stillness: pulse slows,
whispers steal near . . . soft like footfalls on
deep-pile Persians. Time for the dimming
of lamps—that sudden void yawning before
with the abruptness of unbidden thought,
filaments' last blue arcs fading to colorless.

Saffron shadows breach windows—faint
as perception in impermeable space.
In liquid dark a hallway holds its breath
pressing in as passing cars spill amber cels
in slo-mo sequences across bedroom walls—
strips from early moving-picture studies.

Ghostly angles and secreted corners hint
of the dead whose habitat they'd been—
hints that entice, inveigle us, unsettling
the ash and leaf mold of past lives,
motion intuiting what eyes can't see—
unwavering—with never a stubbed toe.

Abstraction seems no longer mere abstract:
refractions, hesitant forays into
desiccated years . . . then blood and spew
splashing the retina—blood that won't be
stanched . . . that one wouldn't stanch . . .
its spill welling truth, time's validation.

Deferral: Dublin Snug

You tell me this is Brendan's Day
yet lorries 'll make refuse rounds,
'chutists plunge into the glide paths
of BritAir flights, and squirrels
suspend stashes against winter?
Why then do shamrock pinlights jig
despite daylight's bright inflections,
terror and doubt invade our thoughts
while sirens shriek futile alarm?

Down the bar "the daily's" called for
as a Guinness tap coughs dry: perch
or peachy skillet chicken—cloves,
just a grating of cinnamon. Rust and
mauve spritz parched sky; to come
muddled in circular reasoning's likely—
so abjure mind-bending eschatology.
Up against the Great Wall. Any day
now . . . change is gonna fall on me.

Infernal Night

(Tristan und Isolde)

Damned within these hell-heat reaches
despair like a Going-Out-of-Business sale
contrary to the Gospel promise fiercer
the higher one goes: this uppermost tier
of Covent Garden, its on-stage brace
two XXLs belaboring their longing
from opposite wings—never to kiss or
embrace the (sometimes) hell of love—
sweat tickling droplets down my back
and my season's companion, my Dante,
with a hesitant sidelong glance asking
where I have led him, why this path
midway through his life's journey, as
the two outsized voices blaze through
hour upon hour (in this stygian heat)
to plight a troth they can never seem
to resolve, let alone consummate.
Outside (in the light from distant stars)
cooler air stirs; here ever more sodden
octaves struggle through infernal night.

Open Head: Eject

Because painting is visceral motion
like a pelican's maw set on overdrive
green gorging on the passing breeze—
small maelstrom in the midst of calm;
yet no desert flowers bloom here only
this default mad pursuit where taproots
steal insistent ways through the stygian
dark, light—Holy Moldy!—angling its
clandestine way. How many shadows
can a man's head cast? Layered thought
would never perch atop those cropped
crepe myrtles nor iron bars inhibit, cells
thrown open on these narrow passages
letting us spy on the new guy's shower—
and each night's slogged hours tolled
by clubs slow-rattled across the bars,
beams prying to ferret out our solace.

Aegean Skirmish

An anguished chant . . . stressed-out, pitiful
shears leaden stillness. Artemis stirs, wakens
at her disciples' wailing, their pleas for succor,
for sustenance—
                     caught in this skirmish
of deities being born, passing away: Christianity,
barred from Ephesus, launches an epistolary
foray against the old faith's waning traditions,
                 its dwindling priestly cadre.

Stone-faced Zeus (bemused) observes the fray
as Apollo mulls duty toward his mediatrix/sister;
Saturn, estranged, turns to tend his groves.
Across the Aegean diamonds of light skitter
water so clear gods might mistake Ephesus for
the precincts of Helicon.
                   Bougainvillea tongues
on nearby hillsides whisper October oracles,
sun scours a high sky; nature validates divinity—
waxing or waning it mayn't, needn't judge.

Another skirmish in history's religious strife:
two idolatries constructing/deconstructing,
seductive appeals which wane to echoes
(as a Woody Allen character once remarked
if Jesus were to hear what's being preached
in His name, He couldn't stop throwing up).
So each age wails calling/seeking/awaiting

the latest *slouching toward Bethlehem to be born*
even as it may already have been and gone.

From suffering the Ancients surmised:
Live a respectful distance from your gods.
Pour their libations.
Don't let them usurp your peace of mind.

No Landscape

There is no landscape for this gesture—
swept offline in the last great storm.

There is only the gloved fist, unshaken
not stirred,
the myopic eye turning inward.
There is only the covetous mind.

A fortuitous meld of effort and luck—
branches' skreak across windowpanes
a basso profundo of wind
the shrill chirrup of katydids—
thought threading haltingly
along ganglia
stalking the bird and its song.

If an icon of truth became manifest
those few not yet numbed
would be discomfited
turning faces from the setting sun.

Birds make song in another galaxy.
Hope is a pigeonholed formulary,
faith a narcissistic cocktail.

There is no landscape for this gesture.

.

Always/ Never

Always is never
whatever we're taught.

Dare to presume. Hope.
Though maybe harbored

in that place we assert
permanence resides

that inner ingle
bowered and fortified.

Born in America we hear
at every turn its mantras:

exceptionalism is reality
father knows best

land of the pilgrims' pride;
but our blood spilled

(even blood has its
expiration date)

sluices out sludge
obliges us to seek

truth in quiet places.
Inward: that ingle

where we uncover
always to be never.

Sudden Sodden

October's turn is inhospitable,
its sudden sodden yellowed leaves
half drowned in days of pelt, gusted
shrieks loosing summer's great valve
to close it off, bright autumn clarity
an iffy aftermath, rotogravure grays
and browns the surer bet. Our host
has proved brusque, anxious for
his guests to be gone: his door thrown
open, then bolted abruptly behind.
Where to go? Batten down, bide days
which drop a scrim on nature, wait
for the scrim to be drawn again; life
works its will even in murk. As grief
and pain, weathered, bring about hope,
as anger dissolved in time dissipates,
as passion waning taps a deeper well,
seasons are fulfilled in both dark
and light. Cereal turns to mulch, the
great valve turns two ways, the bridge
of change is only the passage across.

Poteen

The way he all at once is there
beside me, stealthily across
the lounge's great parabola
footfalls muffled in carpet pile;

says Tom, "I've scanned the book
for who's in the house tonight; seems
you're the only one with promise."
(His little joke; he knows me from

two former Ballykilty stays.)
A sly half-smile his birthright, adds,
"Tell me now, have ya had poteen?"
as if I might have come on it—

Eire's moonshine, untaxed spirits
not on offer at any pub.
Next thing I know I'm soft-shoeing
alongside Tom; at the long bar—

Victorian-imposing—Tom
ducks below, hoists a clear bottle
from depths unearthed, bears it toward
the dark, sheltered ingle unseen,

fills two liqueur glasses half-way,
then toasts, cautions, "mind: a sip."

I take no more than coats my tongue;
in moments it seems my brain-case

comes unhinged, thought sails free
of its moorings and skims over
the room. Snatches of small talk
jigsaw surrealistically.

I'm an observer of myself
from above, able to converse
with Tom, but neither direct nor
impose sense on what I say.

In my interlude, an unknown
door swings open on mysteries
unfathomed; Tom's shamanistic
gaze hints truths he mayn't voice.

Moments later my transport ends;
the lounge resumes its usual mien.
Yet a few stray insights linger,
glimmers not to be swept away.

Solace

French roast coffee in lifting light
tart dark mother eking early solace

summoning steam-drift of reverie
night's slow-stoked vision peeling—

dim as a radial passageway along
the Grand Bazaar tunneling to day's

yet uncovered mysteries—not so as
to trigger-cock nerves like a roadside

detonator ticking stealthily—but as
red-flash cardinals peep bright-note

one-note like an old percolator
pip-blip-pip-blip funneling up while

plane trees joust with the braving sun
shouldering big-limbed into morning.

***

Three flights up the old wooden fort
Ankara spills beneath its balcony:

to lunch on Turkish pizza—not for
the squeamish—overripe meat with

wine to dull (much of) our revulsion;
a breeze lifts across October, a hint

of freshness far from Istanbul's chaw:
commuter vans' choking exhausts,

coffee in combat with smog as old men
early at their newspapers and chess

sip from demitasses thick as lentil soup.

To an Anole

al memoria de Pablo Neruda

Deep-browed—
observant—
you crouch
on watch as I
pass the gate
eyeing me
as you eye life
stoically mute.

The tail you lost
a long-gone day
regenerates.
And why not life?
And you go on
to eye another age
blood warmed
by sunlight

of another time
and by beauty
all around—
beauty always
all around—
that you'd wish
your heart larger
to encompass.

Venereal Soil

Cardinals cleave dawn as if parting the Red Sea;
the sun brightens into their pips, warms them
as they splash their morning bathe; sky-sweep's
a Huddle House griddle scoring parched earth.
We know why the Seminoles wept and flew
before the first onslaught of beachcombers
probing for buried pelf with sonic toys,
hordes of miniature golfers' smaller minds—
paved paradise . . . put up a parking lot.

All seems benign to the newly encamped:
they conjure golden sand, fountains of youth,
while we like Crusoes scan for lost Fridays
who stole across the dunes decades ago
and haven't returned. Maybe it's just as well:
they'd stumble on strip malls and lose their way,
ears haunted by the music of the spheres—
chaff of its harmony all that lingers.

(Sand)spurs

Florida's a frightful place: we have
Tyrannosaurus Rex as governor
and an obeisant legislature tucked
into that town abandoned by irony
sustained on pork rinds and Co-Cola.

Our residents are either too busy
scratching a living from sandspurs
or competing in shuffleboard matches
(Henry VIII loved the game, at which
he lost £9 to a Lord William in 1532)
and miniature golf to become engaged.

Snowbirds just check the sun's angle
adjusting beach lounges accordingly.
Lucky them; we're due to sweat it out
until October—and (damn!) there
goes my disc again, careening out of
the scoring area—
                    so I may as well
write the Gov my disgruntled letter;
I suppose an aide will read it to him.

Admiral Motel & Taxidermy

(Ocala, FL)

Turnoffs & crossroads break the highway;
at intervals spurs sever the right-of-way.
Scatters of pitch pine swallow sunlight
and vines wrestle traffic lanes for primacy.
Featureless, rust-gray flats—crazed clay—
only the soaring hawks seem to spy logic
in this topography. And they're likely
faking it. Among finger paint squiggles
of brush the motel emerges, bleached buff,
in an edgy truce with the rhododendrons.
Varicose-vein clouds streak the pallid sky;
suffocating heat claws at each drawn breath.
                    *   *   *
I'd posit suicide before homicide—possibly
plea-bargain down to euthanasia: fingers—
arms even—brittled in this heat too readily
snap off (no fault). Makes work chancier.
Take this one: spent his night in number 7.
Who'd've guessed he'd shrivel so with all that
girth scraped away? Gonna take a deal of
padding to ready him for display. Odd how
each one poses his special challenge; I'd say
no amount of book study'd prepare a person

for such conditions: book 'em in, skin 'em,
stuff and mount. Sure makes for active days.

The Barn

All hell's broken loose with a skreak like
hinge screws working loose in old wood.
My friend Matt's the entertainer tonight
at Pawlet's social center and watering hole,
singing in his deep, whisky-mellow voice,
accompanying himself on his guitar. But
Matt's been stoking with beer right along—
a shot or two probably as well—and he's
well into his second set.
                              A few regulars
are growing restless, anxious for the old
favorites they're shouting for; Matt's glad
to oblige, but the manager's getting on him
for spicing his lyrics with f- and s- bombs.
From where I sit, triangulation makes it
hard to sort out, but after a few warnings
the manager orders Matt off the stage;
he's going, with loud protests of innocence.

The customers have turned on the manger,
and there's a do-all like what you see when
baseball dugouts empty—dust-ups, fists
cocked, shoulder rolls, no punches landed.
Matt's repaired to the bar, where I join him;

his sly smile's all I need to tell me: time to
quit entertaining, and get on getting oiled.

Uncle Joe

We had this Uncle Joe who lived in Troy:
he'd gone more Irish with the years—even
developed a brogue—but he came by it
honestly, looking as he did like he'd just
fallen off a shamrock (which I'm sure he had,
in his cups, more than a time or two). Weekdays
he rose at 5 for the Ford Motor Plant, so come
Saturday he'd be up before 7 to the Notty Pine,
down the way, for the Saturday Eye Opener—
a shot of rye and a beer for a quarter. After
a couple or three with his mates, he'd head home
to breakfast. "Maesie," he'd call, "I'm famished."
From breakfast to noon was a nap, then lunch,
and then he'd ready for The Mowing of the Lawn.
"Boys," he'd say, "grab yourselves a quart beer;
we'll go out to the side porch and watch my lazy,
good-for-nothing son cut the grass." On any
Saturday Joe couldn't put away a dozen quarts,
Aunt Mae would fret that "Joe must be feeling
a bit peckish." My brother Terry's wedding
reception was at our family home. We served up
drink and non-alcoholic punch—but Joe took care
of the punch when no one was around, tipping
a pint of whisky into it. In the kitchen the men
grew louder where the whisky poured out neat.

Joe's rasp carried above all. Aunt Mae went out to ask Joe to lower his voice: "Joseph—think of the neighbors." Striding into the sitting room Joe threw up the sash, leaned forth, and "neighbors" he shouted out, "Maesie—fuck the neighbors!"

Pius, My Man

Here in the papal apartments (nice digs!)
with my old childhood pal Pacelli.
Now that he's snagged the triple tiara
he's even more uptight than ever
(ah, those beer hall days in old Berlin!).
"So," I begin, "Eugenio . . . Gino . . . Pius,
my man." The gaze. Through those
steel-rimmed glasses. "Your holi . . ."
sotto voce. "Come on, your holiness, stir up
a spell for me, you know, for old-times'
sake. Some o' that old white magic—say, like

Eye of newt, and toe of frog,
Wool of bat, and tongue of dog,
And I on the opposite shore will be
Ready to ride and spread the alarm . . ."

He dead-pans me: that thin-lipped smile
that gives nothing away. The progeny
of Vatican diplomats, himself the thing—
diplomacy—itself. And how Herr Hitler
laughed and twitched his mustache, that
stage har-har of his! at Gino's sly/shy
attempts at humor. AH got the last laugh,
of course, inking those Vatican Accords.
So now my old buddy rides his sedata
around his little kingdom, Swiss Guards
and all, while The Chancellor stirs up

a world of trouble. But if thin lips can
trip up a tyrant, my man Pius' surely will.

"Pricing the Diamond (or Emerald)"

(for Frank O'Hara)

Ah, Frank! you wouldn't have outlived
your time, your nerve's magnetic North:
you couldn't know what exit the Fates
held in store—*just a plaything of the gods,
and all that*—but had you, would you have
played it any other way? I'm sure not:
gone, you needn't scheme to outreach,
extend the boundaries of the little world
you'd helped enliven, cobbled together
(stepping onstage before your entrance cue,
exiting too soon, in your hoarse whisper)
nor fall mute before youthful acolytes,
your fierce flame guttering, burnt low,
à la recherché du temps perdu.

On Mozart's Requiem

Death hymn to light eternal
Its/life's inherent paradox

Crying in its plaintive key
Et lux perpetua luceat eis

While each day light unfolds
And carries to its porch joy

To those who are
Open to its fleeting gift,

Intermittent and transient;
Of it what do we heedless

Let slip away, eluding us
Even as we grope greedily

For its counterfeit forms—
The vessel departing its dock

While we gaze myopically
Too distracted even to glance

Toward its westward retreat:
Et lux perpetua luceat eis.

Sparrow at My Doorstep

Gratuity of the cat that prowls my yard
insinuating himself between, beneath
tangles of tropical growth
you seem to doze
as if you might rouse yourself
from a brief bird nap—
breast feathers unruffled, one wing
fanned under like a hammock—
but still with a stillness no sleep
in nature ably apes.

I've heard you—in the shrill chorus—
where the prowler stalked life;
now his stealth has stilled you.
And he, true to the life in him
has taken life. But more:
he's placed his trophy, mocking sleep,
at my doorstep to let me know
what a good cat he is—
to implicate me in his life by
implicating me in your death.

The Meaning of Is

An apple recumbent
on a desktop
its aroma, color—
red or its perception?

Firmness of flesh
or its inflection:
texture—absent
taste—who can say?

On a desktop
enveloped by space—
what force
maintains a sphere?

Along Fifth Avenue
at a crosswalk
a curbside gathering—
what jostles, what vectors?

Who at the curbside
might conjure an apple
recumbent on a desk—
its texture, its tartness?

Everything depends on
the apple's pith

everything depends on
the meaning of is.

Imperative

Tobacco juice light spits through the overcast:
sunstrike webs the slash pines and drips from
dogwoods onto a few parched rhododendrons.
The sulfurous stink from a Georgia Pacific mill
congeals humidity. I-95 hurries between these
slack, bruised towns, its shoulders pollen crusted
as thick as rime on an old diner coffee pot,
punctuated "RIP" and "Jesus Saves" by crude
crosses wound with baling wire and sun-bleached
never-dies sanctified in gullies of swamp-run.

The sky's a boil suppurating neglect beneath
which a hand-lettered sign asserts "Pick Up
Hitchhikers!" Only stirring swamp grass around.
Who posted this imperative? His voice so faded
one hears only the susurrus of lonely grass?
So pale he's just this weathered sign, no more
than a ghost-conjured hand, its thumb thrust
toward the elsewheres it might ache to see
far from this last-chance no-place stretch even
the highway's hot-footing it to leave behind.

Shame

Painful memories caustic,
shaming, locked in a trunk,
taken to the attic, secreted
behind, beneath discards
to gather decades of dust—
but there never is, never
can be enough abrasion
in time to rub off shame,
to insulate against the ache
of recollections seeping to
worry (again) from webs &
clots into my unwary wits.

Restoration

Manchester spring—this scented light—
and as ever-long Equinox backdrops
shimmering air: lilies broach a boundary
fence to tongue sparks of torquing sun;
bees keep immemorial pacts with clover
to harvest June, gathering its sweetness.
Pellucid beams Hockney-score electric
webs darting the pool's length, brightness
so intense it distills a gold selvage
from cumulonimbus' tumbling folds.
Birches' mottled whites flare; their leaves
tumble, sporting a carnival of hues
to warm applause—a standing O to day—
as willows kite The Wave, balsams
scattering radiant attar. Mountains
crowd close as if to shelter the valley;
each tree, sharp-etched, stands out along
foothills and across peaks' summits.
Plunge now into the pool's cold depths,
day's freshness clarity refined; restore
from springs your stress-harried mind.

Hayfield

A hayfield stretches
beyond the scope

the keen-eyed sweep
of a boy's vision

but not beyond his
image-fashioning.

Reason may rein
vision's keen aim

to loose its élan
its fluid grace

to dance buttercups
& Queen Anne's Lace

skate the birch leaves'
silvered sleeves

swing across branches'
bowsprit arcs.

His world's not bounded
by a hayfield

but in its sweep
a boy can learn

much of what he will
value for life.

Clarity

He walked into the field.
Brilliance was all around defining,
illumining every particular
etching each wildflower flaring
with a clarity almost inspired
that united him with the motif,
a oneness he intuited but had
no impulse, no need, to name
as he wandered the tall grass.

He hiked as a force seemed
to impel him through timeless light
washing through him.
His spirit was joy though he sought
no words for what he felt,
for what he seemed to intuit.

Light's intensity waned as he
traversed more deliberately
the way he'd journeyed.
As the last of summer day
passed behind the mountain
he envisioned how this day
might be succeeded by others
that would guide him nearer
the ineffable.

He couldn't know that his vision
this day would be recalled
only in diminishing insight,
that its brilliance would never again
infuse him, that this random,
unsought illumination
had begun to dim
even as he inhabited
the joy of clarity's light.

Caught Breath

The frayed Montgomery Ward towel that
I lap-robe to repel *NYTimes* print props
The Collected Poems of Frank O'Hara
at an angle for reading; dark, clotted storm
clouds overlay a scrubbed-air afternoon,
oak trees stirring, leaking intervals of light.

Past my front porch a young hunk leads
his loitering Jack Russell terrier, dapple
strobing his broad shoulders, down pecs
and abs, sparking off green-frame glasses.
The pantry door—I'm sure I'd closed—
springs open with an oarlock's click:
spirit of black beans, hear my orisons!
Respond in the patois of your ancestors,
bless from your flickering mirage, ritual
sparking a dying charge—then snuffed.

My breath catches: a tight-throat fantasy
of have-been might-have-beens, of each
day's death another fireball eaten by
ocean. If I'd not sought New York—
or it me—I'd have withered away in that
spot-on mid-south-cliché college town.
Frank O'Hara had it nailed: *I can't even
enjoy a blade of grass unless I know there's*

a subway handy, or a record store or some
other sign that people do not totally regret *life.*

I'd rather repudiate regret than live it:
Thoreau's *quiet desperation* ends in the
febrile stirring of tea leaves; instead seek
your inner New York—a koan each day
breath vitalizes the spirit that persists
now . . . where's that dog walker gotten?

Lethargy(4/21/13)

It's unseemly unseasonably sharp
        for April & when you sharpen
pencils too vigorously you end up
        with a mound of shavings;

threatened rain doesn't fall
        though the sky looks pregnant
& I don't imagine putting it off
        will render this poem any finer.

The 8:47 egret glides in all flash
        & hauteur his vaudevillian strut
a self-important maitre d's:
        perhaps you'd care to peruse our carte
of luncheon specials—luncheon

        not lunch—& btw those lizards
tucked into the long-leafed liriope
        look appealing; he launches his
hypnotic neck-sway. If the sun

        isn't about to break through
I guess I'll have to make do, leaf
        through old poetic favorites &
Manhattan stardust memories.

Falling in Love Again

I have a small oil painting my aunt
bought years ago: in soft June light
a Vermont hillside, a majestic elm.

For years it hung above family dinners
so high on the wall that as children
we had to crane our necks to see.

It had grown dusty, shabby and sad.
Its frame had gone chipped and dull.
It didn't draw even a second glance.

It went—hillside and elm—to the garage.
At times I meant to toss it; it scarcely
seemed worth a walk to the dumpster.

On impulse one day I took off its frame.
On impulse I brushed off layered dust.
I allowed the painting another look.

In porch light now it evokes Vermont.
In porch light now the elm tree thrives.
Falling in love again . . . I can't help it.

Après-Mike, 2003

On my deck—alone in October's sharp—
I recollect our ready camaraderie

Martinis refreshing friendship's bonds
my pleasure welling in your company.

Now sunlight through the biting air
quickens rather than chilling me;

unclad branches—hungry children—
stretch toward autumn's emptied pantry;

below me scarlet leaves swirl pirouettes
across the fairways' dappled swells.

Winter nears but I'm not yet willing
to let go summer's tensile strands;

the warmth and joy your visit brought
radiates comfort still—when, abruptly,

serrated gusts pierce my reverie, snatching
sunlight's last friendship-banked content.

Assisted Living

(for John Paul)

The bells are tolling hosannas
sorrow breaks like thick cloud:

He has fallen from a height
but not from a great height.

He is injured, but his injury
is slight; he has possibly been

more injured by his dreams.
He wears no crown of thorns

his body bears no piercings.
Through the grace of those

who minister to his needs
(and by the grace of God)

he has been lifted up, risen.
His sufferings are assuaged;

It is Easter.

Diamond Dust

*Not having seen him in the three games of the Minnesota series,
we're now seeing John in the first two games here.*

Seeing John? Are you? In what sense? You're quite sure?
Because I can't see him, don't see him at all. You may be
experiencing an illusion ... if not, possibly you'd be so
good as to point him out to me. Or perhaps he's been and
gone ... or never has been ... never was? It's a beautiful
evening here in Arlington ... oops ... we're in New York.

Now, with a runner on third, and two out, he finds a hole.

Finds a hole? Where is this hole ... in his sock? In which
sock? Or perhaps there's a rip in his uniform from earlier,
sliding on his steal of the bag (and, by the way, that "bag,"
or base, still seems to be there—I can see *it*—though not
John, whom *you still* claim to see)? Or are you referring to
a metaphorical hole of some sort? And if it's metaphorical,
chimerical, how did "he" (the batter) manage to "find" it?
Is he a kind of savant? Or wordsmith, possibly? Could
this hole, if it's not metaphorical, be found—and verified
existentially—by others? Might it be to their advantage to
do so, or only to this batter's who has managed to find it?

He got all of it ... an upper-deck shot.

53

Now I don't know about anyone else, but I'd have whatever he's having (though if "he got all of it"—literally—I suppose there'd be none left for me or anyone else). But if there is still a bit, I'll certainly go upper-deck: no well drinks for me. I can afford upper-deck, and I'd be pleased to raise a glass to that fellow who got all of it—assuming that's true only in an approximate sense and there's still a shot or two there. Maybe he'd also share some with that fellow who found the hole in his sock: poor bastard needs someone to stand him a drink since he's so down and out. Ditto the guy who's been seen by the play-by-play announcer but eludes the rest of us. In the rosy glow of a couple upper-deck shots, we might all arrive at a moment at which we'd be able to see John.

Aftermath (Times Sq. Shuttle)

(Walker Evens: Subway Passengers, NYC, 1941)

Shock like a slap across my cheek!—
the stunning suddenness of blood-rush
as if—almost—I didn't know that hand
as well as my own. This trip into town
we've made a hundred times ... altered
as by a quick-swiped blade. Look at her:
gangly, just that bit awkward, her wistful
Mona Lisa half-smile and—always—an
over-fussy hat (absurd feathers!) perched
on her head ... Oh, too incongruous!
If this train's unforgiving seats hadn't
sent an ache down the back of my legs
I'd suppose I'd been daydreaming.

> *I didn't choose to tell ... hadn't meant to ...*
> *thought over and over I'd keep it to myself—*
> *that even life-long friendship had its limits*
> *when it came to confidence. Then I began ...*
> *just enough ... half-blurted, half-whispered*
> *against the incessant clatter of the A train*
> *in a shaky voice scarcely my own ... so*
> *I knew I had to go on: she fixed me with*
> *That Look—those steely eyes—pinned me.*
> *Beneath that fur-trimmed hat she glared like*

one of the Furies! My hands in my lap—
clasped tight together in dark gloves—began
to quiver, and quick tears burned my eyes.

The offhanded way she told me … in that
tremulous voice …and her sidelong glance:
all the coffees we've shared in our kitchens
and she couldn't confide to her best friend that
she and Homer had come to a dead-end, that
she needed her "space"? Space? I guess I'll
need to be direct with her. She seems stunned
that she could have brought herself to admit
so much. Her eyes are tearing … I don't think
this is a time for questions … this is a time for
sympathy—no point in spoiling our outing.
At lunch … when we're seated in Schrafft's …
maybe then she'll relax … and tell me more.

I thought she'd be less cold … less disapproving.
That fierce diva look really puts me off! I feel
as if the car is careening, spinning in orbit …
I could never tell her it's Hank. So young, warm.
So unlike Homer. How did I ever snag him?
Or is he just having a fling? And what about me?
I couldn't divorce. My friends wouldn't approve …
even if Hank was inclined to marry … I know
I'm no catch. Still, I'm in love with him—
I suppose—I've never known real passion:
Mother told me passion was sin. You marry

for security, a man you can respect. Mother
wasn't happy with Father. As for Homer,
what's to be happy with? Cold November.

In a few months ... whoever he is ... she'll
be over him. Homer's a provider ... though
God knows he'd send a chill through anyone.
When she breaks it off she'll need her friends
more than ever ... me especially. We share
interests ... window-shopping ... visits to
museums, the Planetarium ... seeing a matinee.
Marge and I go way back. I won't ... can't ...
sacrifice all we've meant to each other. We'd
never find a friendship like ours ... someone to
confide in ... laugh with, cry, share secrets; so
there! Force a smile ... for both our sakes.

Whitney Alfresco

Either this new alfresco café encroaches
pigeons' turf or the pigeons are crowding
the space of increasingly wary patrons—
the birds would have their perspective—
at any rate the prospect of being guano-
pelted seems to have put diners on edge
in this cheerless, cast concrete bunker
the Whitney set up for outdoor dining.

The holiday crowd has stymied service, so
a fledgling maitre d' tries charm to disarm
chatting up a mother whose children perch
gingerly at a hastily-laid table, white
linen and all. Pigeons work patrons ever
more aggressively with most enticing
warbles while competing for every scrap
that falls.
      The maitre d' continues to circle
on a glide path to snuff brush fires, lunches
still not arriving. At a couple of tables
the flap of napkins at verging birds triggers
a responsive dust-up of wings as pigeons
hop and sidestep one another. A singleton

at a corner table bolts abruptly from his seat;
clutching his wine glass, he retreats toward
a tranquil haven. For him this urban
café proved one alfresco too many.

Blizzard of '76

As birds in winter peck for orts
I strain for a hint of your voice
to leaven truth, embers to stir
to thaw this February chill.

I wish the end of love could be
a sudden cauterizing sear—
I wish—but that I know
its lingering, its withering.

My failure to breathe in new life
won't prompt me to rescind our past
in acrid recriminations:
our days still flare in memory.

In snowdrifts wanderers lie down
enveloped in seductive warmth;
anxious I lie—and toss—
in dark hours plumbing solitude.

Clochán (Beehive Huts)

Dingle Peninsula

The Dingle plunges toward a restive sea
its hills mulled sage in mottled light
its myths and legends cloaked in mist.
Everywhere is stone strew of ring forts
whose sentinels held this shore against
invaders—stark flint haunting time—
everywhere cloistered *clochán*, huts
of hermit-monks' green martyrdom
in remote nooks, withdrawn from all
but God's eye. A warming brightness
breaks free, shimmering the turquoise
wave-flocked sheet of the Atlantic.

Up a steep blind beyond a pasture gate
held by a golden haired shepherd—
his hand cupped ready (for a punt)
to ferry travelers to another world—
beehive huts huddle a wildflower rise
with Skellig Michael, the martyrs' crown,
their distant prospect. Fat sheep gnaw
grass tufts where we few curious roam,
sun-struck in wonder—puzzlement—
ill equipped to ferret out the impulse
of those who sought God in such solitude,
ill equipped to emulate their way,
as eastward light casts shadows like

hermits' shapes moving before us
to a place few of us could hope to know.

Procession

Over the last of a fine old Bordeaux
Into our post-dinner musings he thrusts Satan:
"The mind can make a Heaven of Hell,
A Hell of Heaven." I grasp the steering,
Pump the brakes—but my thought veers
From its path, nearly spins out. Loosed by his
Earnest intensity the procession begins.

The power of the Word: all
Acknowledge the power of the Word.

He elaborates his skeptical position
On humanity, citing Schopenhauer:
"We are lambs in a field, sporting
Beneath the eye of the butcher."
He posits the futility of goals
Warming to his theme, pleased—
I note—at his words' serrated edge.

The power of the Word: all
Defer to the power of the Word.

Wraiths and whispers materialize: shadows—
Time-warped refractions from my past—
Waver up Eighth Avenue. Like a sewer rat
Scurrying the maze of recollection
I grope for a telling riposte to his words

My mind numbed by the haunting,
Robotic drift of fleeting images.

The power of the Word: all
Must defer to the power of the Word.

I lack the wit or daring to respond
"It is enough for a man to live
At peace with a few friends" to blunt
His intensity; so I find myself
Arraigned by the specters—who
Assume the posture of judges—
Contentious, haranguing: unsought.

The Word begins to flag:
The power of the Word begins to fail.

The wraiths' gaping mouths hiss censure
Of my timidity; indictment alternates
With ominous silence. The procession fades
Up Eighth Avenue. Nothing is resolved—
Only I catch a faint, trailing echo:
"When you are old, all that will matter
Is how much you have loved."

The power of the Word may fail;
All that will matter is Love.

Acknowledgements

The author is grateful to editors of the following journals, in which a number of poems—some since revised—first appeared:

Crab Orchard Review: "Open Head: Eject"
Crazyhorse: "Lethargy (4/21/13)"
Green Mountains Review: "Infernal Night"
Main Street Rag: "Falling in Love Again"
Pine Island Journal: "Sudden Sodden"
Pleiades: "Quickened Dark"
Polyphon: "Imperative," "Sparrow at My Doorstep," "To an Anole"
Tampa Review: "Discernment"

Thanks to Jay Bridgers for his judicious insights.

www.ingramcontent.com/pod-product-compliance
Lightning Source LLC
Chambersburg PA
CBHW070842050426
42452CB00011B/2382